What are emotions and why do I feel this way?

Nicole Onwuasor is a passionate children's book author who believes in the magic of storytelling. With a heart full of creativity and a love for diverse children's books that inspire and entertain young readers, Nicole has created a series about her family and the experiences they go through together.

As a dedicated wife and mom, family plays a central role in Nicole's life, and it's the joy and wonder in the eyes of her loved ones that fuel the stories she creates. Each book is a testament to the belief that every child deserves a story that sparks their imagination and helps them see the world in new, exciting ways.

When Nicole isn't writing, she loves spending time with her family, traveling, and finding new inspirations for the next adventure to share with young readers.

www.nicoleonwuasor.com